CW00406533

1 MONTH OF
FREE
READING

at

www.ForgottenBooks.com

By purchasing this book you are eligible for one month membership to ForgottenBooks.com, giving you unlimited access to our entire collection of over 700,000 titles via our web site and mobile apps.

To claim your free month visit:

www.forgottenbooks.com/free302159

ISBN 978-0-483-11245-2
PIBN 10302159

ENGLISHMAN

RETURNED FROM PARIS.

BEING THE SEQUEL TO

THE ENGLISHMAN IN PARIS.

A FARCE.

IN TWO ACTS.

As performed at

The Theatres Royal in Drury-Lane and Covent-Garden.

By *SAMUEL FOOTE*, Efq.

A NEW EDITION.

LONDON:

PRINTED FOR W. LOWNDES, N.º 77, FLEET-STREET.

M,DCC,LXXXVIII.

Price One Shilling.

By *Mr. FOOTE.*

OF all the passions that possess mankind,
    The love of novelty rules most the mind,
In search of this, from realm to realm we roam,
Our fleets come fraught with every folly home.
From Lybia's deserts hostile brutes advance,
And dancing dogs in droves skip here from France,
From Latian lands gigantic forms appear,
Striking our British breasts with awe and fear,
As once the Lilliputions———Gulliver,
Not only objects that affect the sight,
In foreign arts and artists we delight,
Near to that spot where Charles bestrides a horse,
In humble prose the place is Charing Cross;
Close by the margin of a kennel's side,
A dirty dismal entry opens wide,
There with hoarse voice, check shirt, and callous hand,
Duff's Indian English trader takes his stand,
Surveys each passenger with curious eyes,
And rustic Roger falls an easy prize;
Here's China porcelain that Chelsea yields,
And India handkerchiefs from Spitalfields.
With Turkey carpets that from Wilton came,
And Spanish tucks and blades from Birmingham,
Factors are forced to favour this deceit,
And English goods are smuggled thro' the street.
The rude to polish, and the fair to please,
The hero of to-night has cross'd the seas,

A 2

Tho'

Tho' to be born a Briton *be his crime,*
He's manufactured in another clime.
'Tis Buck *begs leave once more to come before ye,*
The little subject of a former story,
How chang'd, how fashion'd, whether brute or beau,
We trust the following scenes will fully shew.
For them and him we your indulgence crave,
'Tis ours still to sin on, and yours to save.

EPILOGUE.

EPILOGUE.

SPOKEN

By Mrs. BELLAMY.

*A*MONG *the arts to make a piece go down,*
   And fix the fickle favour of the town.
An Epilogue *is deem'd the fureſt way*
To atone for all the errors of the play ;
Thus when pathetic ſtrains have made you cry,
In trips the Comic Muſe, and wipes your eye,
With equal reaſon, when ſhe has made you laugh,
Melpomene *ſhould ſend you ſniveling off :*
But our Bard, unequal to the taſk,
Rejeſts the dagger, and retains the maſk :
Fain would he ſend you chearful home to-night,
And harmleſs mirth by honeſt means excite ;
Scorning with luſcious phraſe or double ſenſe,
To raiſe a laughter at the fair's expence.
What method ſhall we chooſe your taſte to hit ?
Will no one lend our Bard a little wit ?
Thank ye, kind ſouls, I'll take it from the pit.
The piece concluded, and the curtain down,
Up ſtarts that fatal phalanx, *call'd* The Town :
In full aſſembly weighs our author's fate,
And Surly *thus commences the debate :*
Pray, among friends, does not this poiſoning ſcene
The ſacred rights of Tragedy *profane ?*
If Farce may mimic thus her awful bowl :
Oh fie, all wrong, ſtark naught, upon my ſoul !
Then Buck *cries,* Billy, *can it be in nature ?*
Not the leaſt likeneſs in a ſingle feature.

My Lord, Lord love him, 'tis a precious piece ;
Let's come on Friday night and have a hiss.
To this a peruquier assents with joy,
Parcequ'il affronte les François, oui, ma foi.
In such distress what can the poet do ?
Where seek for shelter when those foes pursue ?
He dares demand protection, sirs, from you.

Dramatis Personæ.

At *C O V E N T - G A R D E N.*

Buck	Mr. *Foote.*
Crab	Mr. *Sparks.*
Lord John	Mr. *White.*
Macruthen	Mr. *Shuter.*
Racket	Mr. *Cushing.*
Tallyhoe	Mr. *Castallo.*
Latitat	Mr. *Dunstall.*
Sergeon	Mr. *Wignel.*
Lucinda	Mrs. *Bellamy.*

La Jonquil, La Loire, Bearnois, and Servants.

THE

ENGLISHMAN

RETURNED FROM PARIS.

ACT I.

Crab *discovered reading.*

AND I do constitute my very good friend, Giles
Crab, *esq. of* St. Martin in the Fields, *executor
to this my will; and do appoint him guardian to my
ward* Lucinda; *and do submit to his direction, the
management of all my affairs, till the return of my
son from his travels; whom I do intreat my said
executor in consideration of our ancient friendship, to
advise, to counsel, &c. &c.*
·John Buck.

A good, pretty legacy! Let's fee, I find myfelf
heir, by this generous devife of my very good
friend, to ten actions at common law, nine fuits
in chancery, the conduct of a boy, bred a booby
at home, and finifhed a fop abroad; together with
the direction of a marriageable, and therefore
an unmanageable wench; and all this to an old
fellow of fixty-fix, who heartily hates bufinefs, is
tired of the world, and defpifes every thing in it.
Why how the devil came I to merit——

Enter

Lat. The defence and offence, the by which, and the whereby, the statute, common and customary, or as *Plowden* classically and elegantly expresses it, 'tis

Mos commune vetus mores, consulta senatus,
Hæc tria jus statuunt terra Britanna tibi.

Crab. Zounds, sir, among all your laws, are there none to protect a man in his own house ?

Lat. Sir, a man's house is his *castellum*, his castle; and so tender is the law of any infringement of that sacred right, that any attempt to invade it by force, fraud, or violence, clandestinely, or *vi et armis*, is not only deemed *felonius* but *burglarius*. Now, sir, a burglary may be committed either upon the dwelling, or out-house.

Crab. O laud ! O laud !

Enter Servant.

Ser. Your clerk, sir——The parties, he says, are all in waiting at your chambers.

Lat. I come. I will but just explain to Mr. *Crab*, the nature of a burglary, as it has been described by a late statute.

Crab. Zounds, sir, I have not the least curiosity.

Lat. Sir, but every gentleman should know——

Crab. I won't know. Besides, your clients——

Lat. O, they may stay. I shan't take up five minutes, sir——A burglary——

Crab. Not an instant.

Lat. By the common law.——

Crab. I'll not hear a word.

Lat. It was but a *clausum fregit*.

Crab. Dear sir, be gone.

Lat. But by the late acts of par ——

Crab.

Crab. Help, you dog. Zounds, fir, get out of my houfe.

Serv. Your clients, fir ———

Crab. Pufh him out [*the lawyer talking all the while*] So, ·ho! · Hark'ee, rafcal, if you fuffer that fellow to enter my doors again, ' I'll ftrip ·and difcard you the very minute.—[*Exit Serv.*]—This is but the beginning of my torments. But that I expect the young whelp from abroad, every in-ftant, I'd fly for it myfelf and quit the kingdom at once.

Enter Servant.

Serv. My young mafter's travelling tutor, fir, juft arrived.

Crab. Oh, then I fuppofe, the blockhead of a baronet is clofe at his heels. Shew him in. This bear-leader, I reckon now, is either the clumfy curate of the knight's own parifh church, or fome needy highlander, the out-caft of his country, who, with the pride of a *German* baron, the poverty of a *French* marquis, the addrefs of a *Swifs* foldier, and the learning of an academy ufher, is to give our heir apparent politenefs, tafte, literature; a perfect knowledge of the world, and of himfelf.

Enter Macruthen.

Mac. Maifter *Crab*, I am your devoted fervant.

Crab. Oh, a *Britifh* child, by the mefs.—Well, where's your charge?

Mac. O, the young baronet is o'the road. I was mighty afraid he had o'er ta'en me; for be-tween *Canterbury* and *Rochefter*, I was ftopt, and robb'd by a highwayman.

Crab. Robb'd! what the devil could he rob you of?

Mac.

Mac. In gude troth, not a mighty booty. *Bu-chanan's* hiſtory, *Lauder* againſt *Melton,* and two pound of high-dried *Glaſgow.*

Crab. A travelling equipage. Well, and what's become of your cub ? Where have you left him ?

Mac. Main you Sir *Charles ?* I left him at *Calais,* with another young nobleman, returning from his travels. But why caw ye him cub, Maiſter *Crab ?* In gude troth there's a meeghty alteration.

Crab. 'Yes, yes,' I have a ſhrewd gueſs at his improvements.

Mac. He's quite a phenomenon.

Crab. Oh, a comet, I dare ſwear, but not an unuſual one at *Paris.* The *Faux*-bourg of *St. Germains,* ſwarms with ſuch, to the no ſmall amuſe-ment of our very good friends the *French.*

Mac. Oh, the *French* were mighty fond of him.

Crab. But as to the language, I ſuppoſe he's a perfect maſter of that.

Mac. He can caw for aught that he need, but he is na quite maiſter of the accent.

Crab. A moſt aſtoniſhing progreſs !

Mac. Suſpend your judgement awhile, and you'll find him all you wiſh, allowing for the ſallies of juvenility ; and muſt take the vanity to myſelf of being, in a great meaſure, the author.

Crab. Oh, if he be but a faithful copy of the admirable original, he muſt be a finiſhed piece.

Mac. You are pleaſed to compliment.

Crab. Not a whit. Well, and what—I ſuppoſe you, and your—what's your name ?

Mac. *Macruthen,* at your ſervice.

Crab. *Macruthen !* Hum ! You and your pupil agreed very well ?

Mac. Perfectly. The young gentleman is of an amiable diſpoſition.

Crab.

Crab. Oh, ay: And it would be wrong to four his temper. You knew your duty better, I hope, than to contradict him.

Mac. It was na for me, Maifter *Crab.*

Crab. Oh, by no means, Mafter *Macruthen*; all your bufinefs was to keep him out of frays; to take care, for the fake of his health, that his wine was genuine, and his miftreffes as they fhould be. You pimp'd for him I fuppofe?

Mac. Pimp for him! D'ye mean to affront—

Crab. To fuppofe the contrary would be the affront, Mr. Tutor. What, man, you know the world. 'Tis not by contradiction, but by compliance, that men make their fortunes. And was it for you to thwart the humour of a lad upon the threfhold of ten thoufand pounds a year?

Mac. Why, to be fure great allowances muft be made.

Crab. No doubt, no doubt.

Mac. I fee, Maifter *Crab*, you know mankind. you are Sir *John Buck's* executor.

Crab. True.

Mac. I have a little thought that may be ufeful to us both.

Crab. As how?

Mac. Could na we contrive to make a hond o'the young baronet?

Crab. Explain.

Mac. Why you, by the will, have the care o'the cafh: and I caw make a fhift to manage the lad.

Crab. Oh, I conceive you. And fo between us both, we may contrive to eafe him of that inheritance which he knows not how properly to employ; and apply it to our own ufe. You do know how.

Mac.

Mac. Ye ha hit it.

Crab. Why what a superlative rascal art thou, thou inhospitable villain! Under the roof, and in the presence, of thy benefactor's representative, with almost his ill-bestowed bread in thy mouth, art thou plotting the perdition of his only child! And, from what part of my life didst thou derive a hope of my compliance with such a hellish scheme?

Mac. Maister *Crab*, I am of a nation——

Crab. Of known honour and integrity; I allow it. The kingdom you have quitted, in consigning the care of its monarch, for ages, to your predecessors, in preference to its proper subjects, has given you a brilliant panegyric, that no other people can parallel.

Mac. Why, to be sure——

Crab. And one happiness it is, that though national glory can beam a brightness on particulars, the crimes of individuals can never reflect a disgrace upon their country. Thy apology but aggravates thy guilt.

Mac. Why, Maister *Crab*, I——

Crab. Guilt and confusion choak thy utterance. Avoid my sight. Vanish!—[*Exit Mac.*]—A fine fellow this, to protect the person, inform the inexperience, direct and moderate the desires of an unbridled boy! But can it be strange, whilst the parent negligently accepts a superficial recommendation to so important a trust, that the person whose wants perhaps, more than his abilities make desirous of it, should consider the youth as a kind of property, and not consider what to make him, but what to make of him; and thus prudently lay a foundation for his future sordid hopes, by a criminal compliance with the lad's

present

prefent prevailing paffions? But vice and folly rule the world.—Without, there!—[*Enter Serv.*] —Rafcal, where d'you run, blockhead? Bid the girl come hither.—Frefh inftances, every moment, fortify my abhorrence, my deteftation of mankind. This turn may be term'd mifantrophy; and imputed to chagrin and difappointment. But it can only be by thofe fools, who, through foftnefs or ignorance, regard the faults of others, like their own, through the wrong end of the perfpective.

Enter Lucinda.

So, what, I fuppofe your fpirits are all afloat. You have heard your fellow's coming.

Luc. If you had your ufual difcernment, fir, you would diftinguifh, in my countenance, an expreffion very different from that of joy.

Crab. Oh, what, I fuppofe your monkey has broke his chain, or your parrot died in moulting.

Luc. A perfon lefs cenforious than Mr. *Crab*, might affign a more generous motive for my diftrefs.

Crab. Diftrefs! a pretty, poetical phrafe. What motive canft thou have for diftrefs? Has not Sir *John Buck's* death affured thy fortune? and art not thou——

Luc. By that very means, a helplefs, unprotected orphan.

Crab. Pho', prithee, wench, none of thy romantic cant to me. What, I know the fex: the objects of every woman's wifh are property and power. The firft you have, and the fecond you won't be long without; for here's a puppy riding poft to put on your chains.

Luc.

Luc: It would appear affectation not to under-
stand you. And, to deal freely, it was upon that
subject I wish'd to engage you.

Crab. Your information was needless; I knew
it.

Luc. Nay, but why so severe? I did flatter
myself that the very warm recommendation of
your deceased friend, would have abated a little
of that rigour.

Crab. No wheedling, *Lucy.* Age and contempt
have long shut these gates against flattery and dif-
simulation. You have no sex for me. Without
preface, speak your purpose.

Luc. What then, in a word, is your advice
with regard to my marrying Sir *Charles Buck ?*

Crab. And do you seriously want my advice?

Luc. Most sincerely.

Crab. Then you are a blockhead. Why where
could you mend yourself? Is not he a fool, a
fortune, and in love?—Look'ee, girl.—[*Enter
Servant*]—Who sent for you, sir?

Ser. Sir, my young master's post-chaise is broke
down, at the corner of the street, by a coal-cart.
His clothes are all dirt, and he swears like a
trooper.

Crab. Ay! Why then carry his chaise to the
coach-maker's, his coat to a scowerer's, and
him before a justice. —— Prithee why dost
trouble me? I suppose you would not meet your
gallant.

Luc. Do you think I should?

Crab. No, retire. And if this application for
my advice, is not a copy of your countenance, a
mask; if you are obedient, I may yet set you
right.

Luc.

Luc. I fhall, with pleafure, follow your direc-
tions. [*Exit.*

Crab. Yes, fo long as they correfpond with
your own inclination. Now we fhall fee what
Paris has done for this puppy. But here he
comes; light as the cork in his heels, or the fea-
ther in his hat.

Enter Buck, *Lord* John, La Loire, Bearnois, *and*
Macruthen.

Buck. Not a word, *mi Lor, jernie,* it is not to be
fupported!—— after being *rompu tout vif,* dis-
jointed by that execrable *pavé,* to be tumbled into
a kennel, by a filthy *charbonnier;* a dirty retailer
of fea-coal, *morbleu!*

Ld. J. An accident that might have happened
any where, Sir *Charles.*

Buck. And then the hideous hootings of that *ca-
naille,* that murtherous mob, with the barbarous—
Monfieur in the mud, huzza! Ah, *pais fauvage,
barbare, inhofpitable!* ah, ah, *qu'eft ce que nous
avons?* Who?

Mac. That is Maifter *Crab,* your father's executor.

Buck. Ha, ha. *Serviteur très humble, monfieur.
Eh bien!* What! is he dumb? *Mac,* my Lor,
mort de ma vie, the veritable *Jack-Roaft-beef* of the
French comedy. Ha, ha, how do you do, *Mon-
fieur-Jack-Roaft-beef,* ha, ha?

Crab. Prithee take a turn or two round the
room.

Buck. A turn or two! *Volontiers. Eh bien!*
Well, have you, in your life, feen any thing fo,
ha, ha, hey!

Crab. Never. I hope you had not many fpec-
tators of your tumble.

B

Buck. *Pourquoi?* Why fo?

Crab. Becaufe I would not have the public curiofity foreftalled. I can't but think, in a country fo fond of ftrange fights, if you were kept up a little, you would bring a great deal of money.

Buck. I don't know, my dear, what my perfon would produce in this country, but the counterpart of your very grotefque figure has been extremely beneficial to the comedians from whence I came. *N'eft ce pas vrai, mi Lor?* Ha, ha.

Ld. J. The refemblance does not ftrike me. Perhaps I may feem fingular; but the particular cuftoms of particular countries, I own, never appeared to me, as proper objects of ridicule.

Buck. Why fo?

Ld. J. Becaufe in this cafe it is impoffible to have a rule for your judgement. The forms and cuftoms which climate, conftitution and government have given to our kingdom can never be tranfplanted with advantage to another, founded on different principles. And thus, though the habits and manners of different countries may be directly oppofite, yet, in my humble conception, they may be ftrictly, becaufe naturally, right.

Crab. Why there are fome glimmerings of common-fenfe about this young thing. Harkee, child, by what accident did you ftumble upon this blockhead?—[*to* Buck]—I fuppofe the line of your underftanding is too fhort to fathom the depth of your companion's reafoning.

Buck. My dear. [*gapes.*]

Crab. I fay, you can draw no conclufion from the above premifes.

Buck. Who I? Damn your premifes, and conclufions too. But this I conclude from what I have feen, my dear, that the *French* are the firft

people

people in the univerfe; that, in the arts of living, they do or ought to give laws to the whole world, and that whofoever would either eat, drink, drefs, dance, fight, fing, or even fneeze, *avec elegance*, muft go to *Paris*, to learn it. This is my creed.

Crab. And thefe precious principles you are come here to propagate.

Buck. *C'eft vrai, Monfieur Crab:* and with the aid of thefe brother miffionaries, I have no doubt of making a great many profelytes. And now for a detail of their qualities. *Bearnois, avancez.* This is an officer of my houfehold, unknown to this country.

Crab. And what may he be?—I'll humour the puppy.

Buck. This is my Swifs Porter. *Tenez vous droit, Bearnois.* There's a fierce figure to guard the gate of an hotel.

Crab. What, do you fuppofe we have no porters?

Buck. Yes, you have dunces that, open doors; a drudgery that this fellow does by deputy. But for intrepidity in denying a difagreeable vifiter; for politenefs in introducing a miftrefs, acutenefs in difcerning, and conftancy in excluding a dun, a greater genius never came from the *Cantons.*

Crab. Aftonifhing qualities!

Buck. *Retirez, Bearnois.* But here's a *bijou*, here's a jewel indeed! *Venez ici, mon cher La Loire. Comment trouvez vous ce Paris ici?*

La L. *Très bien.*

Buck. Very well. Civil creature! This, *Monfieur Crab*, is my cook *La Loire*, and for *hors d'oeuvres, entre rotis, ragoûts, entremets,* and the difpofition of a defert, *Paris* never faw his parallel.

Crab.

Crab. His wages, I·fuppofe, are proportioned to his merit.

Buck. A bagatelle, a trifle.   Abroad but a bare two hundred.   Upon his cheerful compliance, in coming hither into exile with me, I have indeed doubled his ftipend.

Crab. You could do no lefs.

Buck. And now, fir, to compleat my equipage, *regardez Monfieur La Jonquil,* my firft *valet de chambre,* excellent in every thing: but *pour l'ac- commodage,* for decorating the head, inimitable. In one word, *La Jonquil* fhall, for fifty to five, knot, twift, tye, frize, cut, curl, or comb with any *garçon perruquier,* from the land's end, to the Orkneys.

Crab. Why, what an infinite fund of public fpirit muft you have, to drain your purfe, mortify your inclination, and expofe your perfon, for the mere improvement of your countrymen?

Buck. Oh, I am a very Roman for that.   But at prefent I had another reafon for returning.

Crab. Ay, what can that be?

Buck. Why I find there is a likelihood of fome little fracas between us.   But, upon my foul, we muft be very brutal to quarrel with the dear, agreeable creatures, for a trifle.

Crab. They have your affeétions then.

Buck. De tout mon cœur. From the infinite civi- lity fhewn to us, in *France,* and their friendly profeffions in favour of our country, they can never intend us an injury.

Crab. Oh, you have hit their humour to a hair. But I can have no longer patience with the pup- py.   Civility and friendfhip, you booby! Yes, their civility at *Paris,* has not left you a guinea in your pocket, nor would their friendfhip to
your

your nation leave it a foot of land in the univerfe.

Buck. Lord *John*, this is a ftrange old fellow. Take my word for it, my dear, you miftake this thing egregiously. But all you *Englifh* are conftitutionally fullen.—November fogs, with falt boil'd beef, are moft curfed recipes for good-humour, or a quick apprehenfion. *Paris* is the place. 'Tis there men laugh, love, and live! *Vive l'amour! Sans amour, et fans fes defirs, un cœur eft bien moins heureux qu'il ne penfe.*

Crab. Now would not any foul fuppofe that this yelping hound had a real relifh for the country he has quitted?

Buck. A mighty unnatural fuppofition, truly.

Crab. Foppery and affectation all.

Buck. And you really think *Paris* a kind of purgatory, ha, my dear?

Crab. To thee the moft folitary fpot upon earth, my dear.—Familiar puppy!

Buck. Whimfical enough. But come, *pour paffer le tems*, let us, old *Diogenes*, enter into a little debate. Mi Lor, and you, *Macruthen*, determine the difpute between that fource of delights, *ce paradis de plaifir*, and this cave of care, this feat of fcurvy and the fpleen.

Mac. Let us heed them weel, my Lord. Maifter *Crab* has met with his match.

Buck. And firft for the great pleafure of life, the pleafure of the table; ah, *quelle difference!* The eafe, the wit, the wine, the *badinage*, the *perciflage*, the *double entendre*, the *chanfons à boire*. Oh, what delicious moments have I pafs'd *chez madame la duchefse de Barbouliac.*

Crab. Your miftrefs, I fuppofe.

Buck. Who, I! *Fi donc!* How is it poffible

for a woman of her rank, to have a *penchant* for
me? Hey, *Mac.*

Mac. Sir *Charles* is too much a man of honour
to blab. But, to say truth, the whole city of *Paris*
thought as much.

Crab. A precious fellow this!

Buck. Taisez vous, Mac. But we lose the point
in view. Now, *Monsieur Crab,* let me conduct
you to what you call an entertainment. And first,
the melancholy mistress is fixed in her chair,
where, by the bye, she is condemned to do more
drudgery than a dray-horse. Next proceeds the
master, to marshal the guests, in which as much
caution is necessary, as at a coronation, with,
" My lady, sit here," and, " Sir *Thomas,* sit
" there," till the length of the ceremony, with
the length of the grace, have destroyed all appre-
hensions of the meat burning your mouths.

Mac. Bravo, bravo! Did I na' say Sir *Charles*
was a phœnomenon?

Crab. Peace, puppy.

Buck. Then, in solemn silence, they proceed
to demolish the substantials, with, perhaps, an
occasional interruption, of, " Here's to you;
" friends," " Hob or nob," " Your love and
" mine." Pork succeeds to beef, pies to pud-
dings: the cloth is removed: madam, drenched
with a bumper, drops a curtesy, and departs;
leaving the jovial host, with his sprightly compa-
nions, to tobacco, port, and politics. *Voilà un*
repas à la mode d'Angleterre, Monsieur Crab.

Crab. It is a thousand pities that your father
is not a living witness of these prodigious improvements.

Buck. C'est vrai. But *à propos,* he is dead, as
you say, and you are ———

Crab.

Crab. Againſt my inclination, his executor.

Buck. Peut être; well, and ——

Crab. Oh, my taſk will ſoon determine. One article, indeed, I am ſtrictly enjoined to ſee performed; your marriage with your old acquaint-ance *Lucinda.*

Buck. Ha, ha, la petite Lucinde ! *& comment.*—

Crab. Prithee, peace, and hear me. She is bequeathed conditionally, that if you refuſe to marry her, twenty thouſand pounds; and if ſhe rejects you, which I ſuppoſe ſhe will have the wiſdom to do, only five.

Buck Reject me! Very probable, hey, *Mac!* But could we not have an *entrevüe ?*

Crab. Who's there ? Let *Lucinda* know we ex-pect her.

Mac. Had na' ye better, Sir *Charles,* equip yourſelf in a more ſuitable garb, upon a firſt viſit to your miſtreſs ?

Crab. Oh, ſuch a figure and addreſs can derive no advantage from dreſs.

Buck. Serviteur. But, however, *Mac's* hint may not be ſo *'mal à propos. Allons, Jonquil, je m'en vais m'habiller.* Mi Lor, ſhall I treſpaſs upon your patience ? My toilet is but the work of ten minutes. *Mac,* diſpoſe of my domeſtics *à leur aiſe,* and then attend me with my portfeuille, and read, while I dreſs, thoſe remarks I made in my laſt voyage from *Fontainbleau* to *Compeigne,*

Serviteur, Meſſieurs ;
Car le bon vin
Du matin
Sortant du tonneau,
Vaut bien mieux que
Le Latin
De toute la Sorbonne,   [Exit.
                                             Crab.

Crab. This is the moſt conſummate coxcomb! I told the fool of a father, what a puppy *Paris* would produce him; but travel is the word, and the conſequence, an importation of every foreign folly: and thus the plain perſons and principles of old *England,* are ſo confounded and jumbled with the excrementitious growth of every climate, that we have loſt all our ancient characteriſtic, and are become a bundle of contradictions; a piece of patch-work; a mere harlequin's coat.

Ld. J. Do you ſuppoſe then, ſir, that no good may be obtained———

Crab. Why, prithee, what have you gained?

Ld. J. I ſhould be ſorry my acquiſitions were to determine the debate. But do you think, ſir, the ſhaking off ſome native qualities, and the being made more ſenſible, from compariſon of certain national and conſtitutional advantages, objects unworthy the attention?

Crab. You ſhew the favourable ſide, young man: but how frequently are ſubſtituted for national prepoſſeſſions, always harmleſs, and often happy, guilty and unnatural prejudices!—Unnatural!—For the wretch who is weak and wicked enough to deſpiſe his country, ſins againſt the moſt laudable laws of nature; he is a traitor to the community, where providence has placed him; and ſhould be denied thoſe ſocial benefits he has rendered himſelf unworthy to partake. But ſententious lectures are ill calculated for your time of life.

Ld. J. I differ from you here, Mr. *Crab.* Principles that call for perpetual practice, cannot be too ſoon received. I ſincerely thank you, ſir, for this communication, and ſhould be happy to have always near me ſo moral a monitor.

Crab.

Crab. You are indebted to *France* for her flattery. But I leave you with a lady, where it will be better employed.

Enter Lucinda.

Crab. This young man waits here, till your puppy is powdered. You may afk him after your *French* acquaintance. I know nothing of him; but he does not feem to be altogether fo great a fool as your fellow.   [*Exit.*

Luc. I'm afraid, fir, you have had but a difagreeable *tête-à-tête.*

Ld. J. Juft the contrary, madam. By good fenfe, tinged with fingularity, we are entertained as well as improved. For a lady, indeed, Mr. *Crab's* manners are rather too rough.

Luc. Not a jot; I am familiarized to 'em, I know his integrity, and can never be difobliged by his fincerity.

Ld. J. This declaration is a little particular, from a lady who muft have received her firft impreffions in a place remarkable for its delicacy to the fair-fex. But good fenfe can conquer even early habits.

Luc. This compliment I can lay no claim to. The former part of my life procured me but very little indulgence. The pittance of knowledge I poffefs, was taught me by a very fevere miftrefs, adverfity. But you, fir, are too well acquainted with Sir *Charles Buck,* not to have known my fituation.

Ld. J. I have heard your ftory, madam, before I had the honour of feeing you. It was affecting: you'll pardon the declaration; it now becomes interefting. However, it is impoffible I

fhould

fhould not congratulate you on the near approach of the happy cataftrophe. ·

Luc. Events that depend upon the will of another, a thoufand unforefeen accidents ʾmay interrupt.

Ld. J. Could I hope, madam, your prefent critical condition would acquit me of temerity, I fhould take the liberty to prefume, if the fuit of Sir *Charles* be rejeƈted——

Enter Crab.

Crab. So, Youngfter! what I fuppofe you are already praƈtifing one of your foreign leffons. Perverting the affeƈtions of a friend's miftrefs, or debauching his wife, are mere peccadilloes, in modern morality. But at prefent you are my care. That way ·conduƈts you to your fellow-traveller.—[*Exit.* Ld. *J.*]—I would fpeak with you in the library. [*Exit.*

· *Luc.* I fhall attend you, fir. Never was fo unhappy an interruption. What could my lord mean? But be it what it will, it ought not, it cannot concern me; Gratitude and duty demand my compliance with the dying wifh of my benefaƈtor, my friend, my father. But am I then to facrifice all my future peace? But reafon not, rafh girl; obedience is thy province.

Tho' hard the tafk, be it my part to prove
That fometimes duty can give laws to love.

[*Exit.*

: A C T

ACT II.

Buck *at his Toilet, attended by three* Valets de Chambre *and* Macruthen.

Mac. NOtwithſtanding aw his plain dealing, I doubt whether Maiſter *Crab* is ſo honeſt a man.

Buck. Prithee, *Mac,* name not the monſter. If I may be permitted a quotation from one of their paltry poets,

Who is knight of the ſhire repreſents 'em all.

Did ever mortal ſee ſuch *mirroirs,* ſuch looking-glaſs as they have here too! One might as well addreſs oneſelf, for information, to a bucket of water. *La Jonquil, mettez vous le rouge, aſſez. Eh bien, Mac, miſerable!* Hey!

Mac. It's very becoming.

Buck. Aye, it will do for this place; I really could have forgiven my father's living a year or two longer, rather than be compelled to return to this—[*Enter* Ld. *John*]—My dear Lord, *je demande mille pardons,* but the terrible fracas in my chaiſe has ſo *gàtéed* and diſordered my hair, that it required an age to adjuſt it.

Ld. J. No apology, Sir *Charles,* I have been entertained very agreeably.

Buck. Who have you had, my dear Lord, to entertain you?

Ld. J. The very individual lady that's ſoon to make you a happy huſband.

Buck.

Buck. A happy who ? huſband! What two very oppoſite ideas confounded *enſemble!* In my conſcience, I believe there's contagion in the clime, and my Lor is infeɕted. But pray, my dear Lor, by what accident have you diſcovered, that I was upon the point of becoming that happy —Oh, *un mari! Diable?*

Ld. J. The lady's beauty and merit, your in-clinations, and your father's injunɕtions, made me conjeɕture that.

Buck. And can't you ſuppoſe that the lady's beauty may be poſſeſs'd, her merit rewarded, and my inclinations gratified, without an abſolute obe-dience to that fatherly injunɕtion ?

Ld. J. It does not occur to me.

Buck. No, I believe not, my Lor. Thoſe kind of talents are not given to every body. *Donnez moi mon manchon.* And now you ſhall ſee me manage the lady.

Enter Servant.

Ser. Young Squire *Racket.* and Sir *Toby Tallyhoe,* who call themſelves your honour's old acquaint-ances.

Buck. Oh the brutes! By what accident could they diſcover my arrival! My dear, dear Lor, aid me to eſcape this Embarras.

Racket *and* Tallyhoe *without.*

Hoic a boy, hoic a boy.

Buck. Let me die if I do not believe the *Hot-tentots* have brought a whole hundred of hounds with them. But they ſay, forms keep fools at a diſtance. I'll receive 'em *en cérémonie.*

Enter

Enter Racket *and* Tallyhoe.

Tally. Hey boy, hoix, my little *Buck.*

Buck. Monfieur le Chevalier, votre très humble ferviteur.

Tally. Hey.

Buck. Monfieur Racket, je fuis charmé de vous voir.

Rack. Anon what !

Buck. Ne m'entendez vous? Don't you under-ftand *French?*

Rack. Know *French!* No, nor you neither, I think, Sir *Toby,* foregad I believe the papiftes ha bewitch'd him in foreign parts.

Tally. Bewitch'd and transformed him too. Let me perifh, *Racket,* if I don't think he's like one of the folks we ufed to read of at fchool, in *Ovid's Metamorphis;* and that they have turned him into a beaft.

Rack. A beaft! No, a bird, you fool. Lookee, Sir *Toby,* by the Lord *Harry,* here are his wings.

Tally. Hey! ecod and fo they are, ha, ha. I reckon, *Racket,* he came over with the wood-cocks.

Buck. Voilà des véritables Anglois. The ruftic rude ruffians !

Rack. Let us fee what the devil he has put upon his pole, Sir *Toby.*

Tally. Aye.

Buck. Do, dear Savage, keep your diftance.

Tally. Nay, fore George we will have a fcrutiny.

Rack. Aye, aye, a fcrutiny.

Buck. En grace. La Jonquil, my Lor, proteƈt me from thefe pyrates.

Ld. *J.*

Ld. J. A little compaffion, I beg, gentlemen. Confider, Sir *Charles* is on a vifit to his bride.

Tally. Bride! Zounds, he's fitter for a band-box. *Racket,* hocks the heels.

Rack. I have 'em, knight. Foregad he is the very reverfe of a bantam cock; his comb's on his feet, and his feathers on his head. Who have we got here! What are thefe fellows, paftry-cooks?

Enter Crab.

Crab. And is this one of your newly acquired accomplifhments, letting your miftrefs languifh for a——but you have company, I fee.

Buck. O, yes, I have been inexpreffibly happy. Thefe gentlemen are kind enough to treat me, upon my arrival, with what I believe they call in this country, a rout.—My dear Lor, if you don't favour my flight. But fee if the toads a'n't tumbling my toilet.

Ld. J. Now's your time, fteal off; I'll cover your retreat.

Buck. Mac, let *La Jonquil* follow to re-fettle my *cheveux.—Je vous remercie mille, mille fois, mon cher* my I or.

Rack. Hola, Sir *Toby,* ftole away!

Buck. O mon Dieu.

Tally. Poh, rot him, let him alone. He'll never do for our purpofe. You muft know we intend to kick up a riot, to-night, at the play-houfe, and we wanted him of the party; but that fop would fwoon at the fight of a cudgel.

Ld. J. Pray, fir, what is your caufe of contention?

Tally. Caufe of contention, hey, faith, I know nothing of the matter. *Racket,* what is it we are angry about?

Racket.

Racket. Angry about ! Why you know we are to demolifh the dancers.

Tally. True, true, I had forgot. Will you make one ?

Ld. *J.* I beg to be excufed.

Rack. May hap you are a friend to the *French.*

Ld. *J.* Not I, indeed fir. But if the occafion will permit me a pun, tho' I am far from being a well-wifher to their arms, I have no objeƈtion to the being entertained by their legs.

. *Tally.* Aye ! Why then if you'll come to-night, you'll fplit your fides with laughing, for I'll be rot if we don't make them caper higher, and run fafter, than ever they have done fince the battle of *Blenheim.* Come along, *Racket.* [*Exit.*

Ld. *J.* Was there ever fuch a contraft ?

Crab. Not fo remote as you imagine ; they are fcions from the fame ftock, fet in different foils. The firft fhrub, you fee, flowers moft prodigally, but matures nothing ; the laft flip, tho' ftunted, bears a little fruit ; crabbed, 'tis true, but ftill the growth of the clime. Come, you'll follow your friend. [*Exeunt.*

Enter Lucinda, *with a Servant.*

Luc. When Mr. *Crab,* or Sir *Charles,* enquire for me ; you will conduƈt them hither —[*Exit. Serv.*] —How I long for an end to this important inter-view ! Not that I have any great expeƈtations from the iffue ; but ftill, in my circumftances, a ftate of fufpence is, of all fituations, the moft dif-agreeable. But hufh, they come.

Enter

Enter Sir *Charles*, *Macruthen*, Ld. *John*, and *Crab.*

Buck. Mac, announce me.

Mac. Madam, Sir *Charles Buck* craves the honour of kiffing your hand.

Buck. Très humble ferviteur. Et comment fe porte Mademoifelle. I am ravifhed to fee thee, *ma chere petite Lucinde.—Eh bien, ma reine !* Why you look divinely, child. But, *mon enfant*, they have drefs'd you moft diabolically. Why, what a *coiffeufe* muft you have, and, *oh mon Dieu*, a total abfence of rouge. But, perhaps, you are out. I had a cargo from *Deffreney* the day of my departure; fhall I have the honour to fupply you ?

Luc. You are obliging, fir, but I confefs myfelf a convert to the chafte cuftoms of this country, and, with a commercial people, you known, fir *Charles*, all artifice——

Buck. Artifice ! You miftake the point, *ma chere.* A proper proportion of red, is an indifpenfible part of your drefs ; and, in my private opinion, a woman might as well appear, in public, without powder, or a petticoat.

Crab. And, in my private opinion, a woman, who puts on the firft, would make very little difficulty in pulling of the laft.

Buck. Oh, Monfieur *Crab*'s judgment muft be decifive in drefs. Well, and what amufements, what fpeƈtacles, what parties, what contrivances, to conquer father time, that foe to the fair ? I fancy one muft *ennuier confiderablement* in your *London* here.

Luc. Oh, we are in no diftrefs for diverfions. We have an opera.

Buck.

Buck. *Italien*, I fuppofe, *pitoiable*, fhocking, *affommant!* Oh, there is no fupporting their *hi, hi, hi, hi.* Ah, *mon Dieu!* Ah, *chaffé brillant foleil,*

> *Brillant foleil,*
> *A-t-on jamais veu ton pareil?*

There's mufic and melody.

Luc. What a fop!

Buck. But proceed, *ma princeffe.*

Luc. Oh, then we have plays.

Buck. That I deny, child.

Luc. No plays!

Buck. No.

Luc. The affertion is a little whimfical.

Buck. Aye that may be; you have here dramatic things, farcical in their compofition, and ridiculous in their reprefentation.

Luc. Sir, I own myfelf unequal to the controverfy; but, furely *Shakfpeare*—My Lord, this fubject calls upon you for its defence.

Crab. I know from what fountain this fool has drawn his remarks; the author of the *Chinefe Orphan,* in the preface to which Mr. *Voltaire* calls the principal works of *Shakfpeare* monftrous farces.

Ld. J. Mr. *Crab* is right, madam. Mr. *Voltaire* has ftigmatized with a very unjuft and a very invidious appellation the principal works of that great mafter of the paffions; and his apparent motive renders him the more inexcufable.

Luc. What could it be, my Lord?

Ld. J. The preventing his countrymen from becoming acquainted with our author; that he might be at liberty to pilfer from him, with the greater fecurity.

Luc. Ungenerous, indeed!

Buck. Palpable defamation.

C

Luc.

Luc. And as to the exhibition, I have been taught to believe, that for a natural pathetic, and a fpirited expreffion, no people upon earth——

Buck. You are impofed upon, child; the *Lequefne*, the *Lanoue*, the *Grandval*, the *Dumenil*, the *Gauffen*, what dignity, what action! But, *à propos*, I have myfelf wrote a tragedy in *French*.

Luc. Indeed!

Buck. En verité, upon *Voltaire's* plan.

Crab. That muft be a precious piece of work.

Buck. It is now in repetition at the *French* comedy. *Grandval* and *La Gauffen* perform the principal parts. Oh, what an *eclat!* What a burft will it make in the parterre, when the king of *Ananamaboe* refufes the perfon of the princefs of *Cochineal!*

Luc. Do you remember the paffage?

Buck. Entire; and I believe I can convey it in their manner.

Luc. That will be delightful.

Buck. And firft the king.

Ma chere princefs, je vous aime, c'eft vrai ;
De ma femme vous portez les charmants attraits.
Mais ce n'eft pas honnête pour un homme tel que moi,
De tromper ma femme, ou de rompre ma foi.

Luc. Inimitable!

Buck. Now the princefs; fhe is, as you may fuppofe, in extreme diftrefs.

Luc. No doubt.

Buck. Mon grand roy, mon cher adorable,
　　　Ayez pitie de moi ; je fuis inconfolable.

[Then he turns his back upon her, at which fhe in a fury]

　　　　　　　　　　　　　　　Monftre

Monſtre, ingrat, affreux, horrible, funeſte,
Oh que je vous aime, ah que je vous deteſte!

[Then he]

Penſez vous, madame, à me donner la loi,
Votre haine, votre amour, ſont les mêmes choſes
    à moi.

Luc. Bravo!

Ld. J. Bravo, bravo!

Buck. Aye, there's paſſion and poetry, and reaſon and rhime. Oh how I deteſt blood, and blank verſe! There is ſomething ſo ſoft, ſo muſical, and ſo natural, in the rich rhimes of the *theatre François!*

Ld. J. I did not know Sir *Charles* was ſo totally devoted to the *belles lettres*.

Buck. Oh, entirely. 'Tis the ton, the taſte, I am every night at the *Caffé* * *Procope*, and had not I had the misfortune to be born in this curſt country, I make no doubt but you would have ſeen my name among the foremoſt of the *French* academy.

Crab. I ſhould think you might eaſily get over that difficulty, if you will be but ſo obliging, as publicly to renounce us. I dare engage not one of your countrymen ſhall contradiét, or claim you.

Buck. No!—Impoſſible. From the barbarity of my education, I muſt ever be taken for *un Anglois*.

Crab. Never.

Buck. En verité?

Crab. En verité.

Buck. You flatter me.

---

* A coffee-houſe oppoſite the French comedy, where the wits
    aſſemble every evening.

         Crab.

Crab. But common juftice.

Mac. Nay, maifter *Crab* is in the right, for I have often heard the French themfelves fay, Is it poffible that gentleman can be *Britifh ?*

Buck. Obliging creatures ! And you concur with them.

Crab. Entirely.

Luc. Entirely.

Ld. *J.* Entirely.

Buck. How happy you make me ! ·

Crab. Egregious puppy ! But we lofe time. A truce to this trumpery. You have read your father's will.

· *Buck.* No ; I read no *Englifh.* When *Mac* has turned it into *French,* I may run over the items.

Crab. I have told you the part that concerns the girl. And as your declaration upon it will difcharge me, I leave you to what you will call an *ecclairciffement.* Come, my Lord.

Buck. Nay, but Monfieur *Crab,* my Lor, *Mac.*

Crab. Along with us.   [*Exit.*

Buck. A comfortable fcrape I am in ! What the deuce am I to do ? In the language of the place, I am to make love, I fuppofe. A pretty employment !

Luc. I fancy my hero is a little puzzled with his part. But, now for it.

Buck. A queer creature, that *Crab, ma petite.* But, *à propos,* How d'ye like my Lord.

Luc. He feems to have good fenfe and good breeding.

Buck. Pas trop. But don't you think he has fomething of a foreign kind of air about him ?

Luc. Foreign ?

Buck. Aye, fomething fo *Englifh* in his manner.

Luc.

Luc. Foreign, and *Englifh!* I don't compre-
hend you.

Buck. Why that is, he has not the eafe, the *je
ne fçai quoi,* the *bon ton.*—In a word, he does not
refemble me now.

Luc. Not in the leaft.

Buck. Ah, I thought fo. He is to be pitied,
poor devil, he can't help it. But, *entre nous, ma
chere,* the fellow has a fortune.

Luc. How does that concern me, Sir *Charles?*

Buck. Why, *je penfe, ma reine,* that your eyes
have done execution there.

Luc. My eyes execution!

Buck. Aye, child, is there any thing fo extra-
ordinary in that? *Ma foi,* I thought by the vi-
vacity of his praife, that he had already fum-
moned the garrifon to furrender.

Luc. To carry on the allufion, I believe my
Lord is too good a commander, to commence a
fruitlefs fiege. He could not but know the condition of the town.

Buck. Condition! Explain, *ma chere.*

Luc. I was in hopes your interview with **Mr.**
Crab had made that unneceffary.

Buck. Oh, aye, I do recollect fomething of a
ridiculous article about marriage, in a will. But
what a plot againft the peace of two poor people!
Well, the malice of fome men is amazing! Not
contented with doing all the mifchief they can
in their life, they are for intailing their malevo-
lence, like their eftates, to lateft pofterity.

Luc. Your contempt of me, Sir *Charles,* I receive as a compliment. But the infinite obliga-
tions I owe to the man, who had the misfortune
to call you fon, compel me to infift, that in my

prefence,

prefence, at leaft, no indignity be offered to his memory.

Buck. Heydey! What, in heroics, *ma reine!*

Luc. Ungrateful, unfilial wretch! fo foon to trample on his afhes, whofe fond heart, the greateft load of his laft hours were his fears for thy future welfare.

Buck. Ma foi, elle eft folle, fhe is mad, *fans doute.*

Luc. But I am to blame. Can he who breaks through one facred relation, regard another? Can the monfter who is corrupt enough to contemn the place of his birth, reverence thofe who gave him being?——impoffible.

Buck. Ah, a pretty monologue, a fine foliloquy this, child.

Luc. Contemptible. But I am cool.

Buck. I am mighty glad of it. Now we fhall underftand one another, I hope.

Luc. We do underftand one another. You have already been kind enough to refufe me. Nothing is wanting but a formal rejection under your hand, and fo concludes our acquaintance.

Buck. Vous allez trop vite, you are to quick, *ma chere.* If I recollect, the confequence of this rejection is my paying you twenty thoufand pounds.

Luc. True.

Buck. Now that have not I the leaft inclination to do.

Luc. No, fir? Why you own that marriage——

Buck. Is my averfion. I'll give you that under my hand, if you pleafe; but I have a prodigious love for the *Louis'.*

Luc. Oh, we'll foon fettle that difpute; the law——

Buck,

Buck. But, hold, *ma reine.* I don't find that my provident father has precifely determined the time of this comfortable conjunction. So, tho' I am condemned, the day of execution is not fixed.

Luc. Sir !

Buck. I fay, my foul, there goes no more to your dying a maid, than my living a batchelor.

Luc. O, fir, I fhall find a remedy.

Buck. But now fuppofe, *ma belle,* I have found one to your hand ?

Luc. As how ? Name one.

Buck. I'll name two. And firft, *mon enfant ;* tho' I have an irrefiftable antipathy to the conjugal knot, yet I am by no means blind-to your perfonal charms; in the poffeffion of which, if you pleafe to place me, not only the aforefaid twenty thoufand pounds, but the whole *terre* of your devoted fhall fall at your——

Luc. Grant me patience.

Buck. Indeed you want it, my dear. But if you flounce, I fly.

Luc. Quick, fir, your other. For this is—

Buck. I grant, not quite fo fafhionable as my other. It is then, in a word, that you would let this lubberly lord make you a lady, and appoint me his affiftant, his private friend, his *cicifbei.* And as we are to be joint partakers of your perfon, let us be equal fharers in your fortune, *ma belle.*

Luc. Thou mean, abject, mercenary thing: Thy miftrefs ! Gracious heaven ! Univerfal empire fhould not bribe me to be thy bride. And what apology, what excufe could a woman of the leaft fenfe or fpirit make, for fo unnatural a connection !

Buck.

Buck. *Fort bien !*

Luc. Where are thy attractions? . Canſt thou be weak enough to ſuppoſe thy frippery dreſs, thy affeƈtation, thy grimace, could influence beyond the borders of a brothel ?

Buck. *Très bien !*

Luc. And what are thy improvements ? Thy air is a copy from thy barber : For thy dreſs, thou art indebted to thy taylor. Thou haſt loſt thy native language, and brought home none in ex‹ change for it.

Buck. *Extrêmement bien !*

Luc. Had not thy vanity ſo ſoon expoſed thy villainy, I might, in reverence to that name, to which thou art a diſgrace, have taken a wretched chance with thee for life.

Buck. I am obliged to you for that. And a pretty pacific partner I ſhould have had. Why, look'ee child, you have been, to be ſure, very eloquent, and upon the whole, not unentertaining : tho' by the bye, you have forgot, in your catalogue, one of my foreign acquiſitions; *c'eſt-à- dire*, that I can, with a moſt intrepid *ſang froid*, without a ſingle emotion, ſupport all this ſtorm of female fury. But, *adieu, ma belle*. And when a cool hour of refleƈtion has made you ſenſible of the propriety of my propoſals, I ſhall expeƈt the honour of a card.

Luc. Be gone for ever.

Buck. *Pour jamais !* Foregad ſhe would make an admirable aƈtreſs. If I once get her to *Paris*, ſhe ſhall play a part in my piece.   [*Exit.*

Luc. I am aſhamed, this thing has had the power to move me thus. Who waits there ? Dear Mr. *Crab* ——

Enter

Enter Lord John *and* Crab.

Ld. J. We have been unwillingly, madam, silent witnesses to this shameful scene. I blush that a creature, who wears the outward mark of humanity, should be in his morals so much below.—

Crab. Prithee why didst thou not call thy maids, and tofs the booby in a blanket?

Ld. J. If I might be permitted, madam, to conclude what I intended saying, when interrupted by Mr. *Crab*—

Luc. My lord, don't think me guilty of affectation. I believe, I guefs at your generous defign; but my temper is really so ruffled, befides I am meditating a piece of female revenge on this coxcomb.

Ld. J. Dear madam, can I affift?

Luc. Only by defiring my maid to bring hither the tea.—My lord, I am confounded at the liberty, but—

Ld. J. No apology. You honour me, madam.

Crab. And prithee, wench, what is thy fcheme?

Luc. Oh, a very harmlefs one, I promife you.

Crab. Zounds, I am forry for it. I long to fee the puppy feverely punifhed, methinks.

Luc. Sir *Charles*, I fancy, can't be yet got out of the houfe. Will you defire him to ftep hither?

Crab. I'll bring him.

Luc. No, I wifh to have him alone.

Crab. Why then I'll fend him. [*Exit.*

Enter

Enter Lettice.

Luc. Place thefe things on the table, a chair on each fide: very well. Do you keep within call. But hark, he is here. Leave me, *Lettice.*
[*Exit* Lettice.

Enter Buck.

Buck. So, fo, I thought fhe would come to; but, I confefs not altogether fo foon. *Eh bien, ma belle,* fee me ready to receive your commands.

Luc. Pray be feated, Sir *Charles.* I am afraid the natural warmth of my temper might have hurried me into fome expreffions not altogether fo fuitable.

Buck. Ah *bagatelle.* Name it not.

Luc. Voulez-vous du thé, monfieur ?

Buck. Volontiers. This tea is a pretty innocent kind of *beverage ;* I wonder the *French* don't take it. I have fome thoughts of giving it a fafhion next winter.

Luc. That will be very obliging. It is of extreme fervice to the ladies this fide the water you know.

Buck. True, it promotes parties, and infufes a kind of fpirit of converfation, and that—

Luc. En voulez-vous encore ?

Buck. Je vous rends mille graces.—But what has occafioned me, *ma reine,* the honour of your meffage by Mr. *Crab ?*

Luc. The favours I have received from your family, Sir *Charles,* I thought, demanded from me, at my quitting your houfe, a more decent, and ceremonious *adieu,* than our laft interview would admit of.

Buck.

Buck. Is that all, *ma chere?* I thought your flinty heart had. at laſt relented. Well, *ma reine, adieu.*

Luc. Can you then leave me ?

Buck. The fates will have it ſo.

Luc. Go then, perfidious traitor, be gone; I have this conſolation, however, that If I cannot legally poſſeſs you, no other woman ſhall.

Buck. Hey, how, what ? '

Luc. And tho' the pleaſure of living with you is denied me, in our deaths, at leaſt, we ſhall ſoon be united.

Buck. Soon be united in death ? When, child ?

Luc. Within this hour.

Buck. Which way ?

Luc. The fatal draught's already at my heart. I feel it here ; it runs thro' every pore. Pangs, pangs unutterable ! The tea we drank, urged by deſpair and love—Oh !

Buck. Well !

Luc. I poiſon'd.

Buck. The devil !

Luc. And as my generous heart would have ſhared all with you, I gave you half.

Buck. Oh, curſe your generoſity !

Luc. Indulge me in the cold comfort of a laſt embrace.

Buck. Embrace ! O confound you ! But it mayn't be too late. *Macruthen, Jonquil !* phyſicians, apothecaries, oil and antidotes. Oh ! *je meurs, je meurs.* Ah, la diableſſe !   [*Exit.*

Enter Lord John *and* Crab.

Crab. A brave wench. I could kiſs thee for this contrivance.

Ld. *J.*

Ld. J. He really deferves it all.

Crab. Deferves it! Hang him. But the fenfible refentment of this girl has almoft reconciled me to the world again. But ftay, let us fee—Can't we make a further ufe of the puppy's punifhment? I fuppofe, we may very fafely depend on your contempt of him?

Luc. Moft fecurely.

Crab. And this young thing here, has been breathing paffions and proteftations. But I'll take care, my girl fha'nt go a beggar to any man's bed. We muft have this twenty thoufand pound, *Lucy*.

Ld. J. I regard it not. Let me be happy, and let him be——

Crab. Pfha, don't fcorch me with thy flames. Referve your raptures; or, if they muft have vent, retire into that room, whilft I go plague the puppy. [*Exeunt.*

Enter Buck, Macruthen, Jonquil, Bearnois, La Loire, Phyfician, Surgeon. Buck *in a Cap and Night Gown.*

Surg. This copious phlebotomy will abate the inflammation, and if the fix blifters on your head and back rife, why there may be hopes.

Buck. Cold comfort. I burn, I burn, I burn— Ah, there's a fhoot. And now, again, I freeze.

Mac. Aye, they are fymptoms of a ftrong poifon.

Buck. Oh, I am on the rack.

Mac. Oh, if it be got to the vitals, a fig for aw antidotes.

Enter Crab.

Crab. Where is this miferable devil? What's he alive ftill?

Mac.

Mac. In gude troth, and that's aw.

Buck. Oh !

Crab. So you have made a pretty piece of work on't, young man !

Buck. O what could provoke me to return from *Paris* ?

Crab. Had you never been there, this could not have happened.

Enter Racket *and* Tallyhoe.

Rack. Where is he ?—He's dead man, his eyes are fix'd already.

Buck. Oh !

Tally. Who poifon'd him, *Racket ?*

Rack. Gad I don't know. His *French* cook, I reckon.

Crab. Were there a poffibility of thy reformation, I have yet a fecret to reftore thee.

Buck. Oh give it, give it.

Crab. Not fo faft. It muft be on good conditions.

Buck. Name 'em. Take my eftate, my—fave but my life, take all.

Crab. Firft then renounce thy right to that lady, whofe juft refentment has drawn this punifhment upon thee ; and, in which fhe is an unhappy partaker.

Buck. I renounce her from my foul.

Crab. To this declaration you are witneffes. Next, your tawdry trappings, your foreign foppery, your wafhes, paints, pomades, muft blaze before your door.

Buck. What, all ?

Crab. All ; not a rag fhall be referved. The execution of this part of your fentence fhall be affigned to your old friends here.

Buck.

Buck. Well, take 'em.

Tally. Huzza, come *Racket*, let's rummage.

                [*Exeunt* Racket *and* Tallyhoe.

Crab. And, laftly, I'll have thefe exotic at-tendants, thefe inftruments of your luxury, thefe panders to your pride. pack'd in the firft cart, and fent poft to the place from whence they came.

Buck. Spare me but *La Jonquil.*

Crab. Not an inftant. The importation of thefe puppies makes a part of the politics of your old friends, the *French ;* unable to refift you, whilft you retain your ancient roughnefs, they have recourfe to thefe minions, 'who would firft, by unmanly means, fap and foften all your native fpirit, and then deliver you an eafy prey to their employers.

Buck. Since then it muft be fo, *adieu La Jon-quil.*   [*Exeunt* Jonquil *and* Bearnois.

Crab. And now to the remedy. Come forth, *Lucinda.*

    Enter Lucinda *and* Lord John.

Buck. Hey, why did not fhe fwallow the poifon ?

Crab. No ; nor you neither, you blockhead.

Buck. Why, did not I leave you in pangs ?

Buc. Aye, put on. The tea was innocent, up-on my honour, Sir *Charles.* But you allow me to be an excellent aftrefs.

Buck. Oh, curfe your talents !

Crab. This fellow's public renunciation, has put your perfon and fortune in your own power : and if you were fincere in your declaration of being directed by me, beftow it there.

Luc. As a proof of my fincerity, my Lord, re-ceive it.

                        Ld. *J.*

Ld. J. With more tranſport, than Sir *Charles* the news of his ſafety.

Luc. to Buck. You are not, at preſent, in a condition to take poſſeſſion of your poſt.

Buck. What ?

Luc. Oh, you recollect; my Lord's private friend; his aſſiſtant you know.

Buck. Oh, ho !

Mac. But, Sir *Charles,* as I find the affair of the poiſon was but a joke, had na'ye better with-draw, and tack off your bliſters ?

Crab. No, let 'em ſtick. He wants 'em. And now concludes my care. But before we cloſe the ſcene, receive, young man, this laſt advice from the old friend of your father: As it is your happineſs to be born a *Briton,* let it be your boaſt; know that the bleſſings of liberty are your birth-right, which while you preſerve, other nations may envy or fear, but can never conquer or con-temn you. Believe, that *French* faſhions are as ill-ſuited to the genius, as their politics are per-nicious to the peace of your native land.

A convert to theſe ſacred truths, you'll find,
That poiſon for your puniſhment deſign'd
Will prove a wholeſome medicine to your mind.

[Exeunt omnes.

F I N I S.

BOOKS, PAMPHLETS, &c. lately published by W. LOWNDES.

1. BARBARIAN CRUELTY ; or Sufferings of Britiſh Captives in Morocco, 1 vol. ſmall 8vo. Price 3s. 6d.
2. BOYLE's VOYAGES and ADVENTURES in ſeveral Parts of the World, 1 vol. 12mo. Price 3s.
3. BROWN's FAMILY TESTAMENT and SCHOLAR's ASSISTANT, in one large volume 12mo. Price 2s.
4. FOOTE's DRAMATIC WORKS, with Memoirs of his LIFE, in 4 vols. 8vo. Price 1l. 10s.
5. FRANKLIN's SOPHOCLES, 1 vol. 8vo. Price 7s.
6. GEOGRAPHY for YOUTH ; illuſtrated by 12 Maps and other Copper-plates, in 1 vol. 12mo. Price 3s. 6d.
7. GUIDE to Stage Coaches, Mails, Waggons, Carts, Coaſting Veſſels, &c. in crown 8vo. Price 1s. ſewed.
8. HERALDRY in MINIATURE, illuſtrated by above 1000 Engravings of Arms, &c. 1 vol. 12mo. Price 3s.
9. HUGHES's LETTERS of Abelard and Eloiſa, with ſeven Poems, and 6 elegant plates, 1 vol. ſmall 8vo. Price 5s. Another Edition, with 6 Plates, in 1 vol. 12mo. 2s. 6d. and a third Sort, with 3 Plates, in foolſcap 8vo. Price 1s. 6d.
10. LONDON DIRECTORY ; or Names and Places of Abode of the Merchants, Traders, &c. of London and its Environs, in crown 8vo. Price 1s. ſewed.
11. LOVE in the EAST ; or Adventures of Twelve Hours. A Comic Opera of three Acts, written by James Cobb, Eſq. in 8vo. Price 1s. 6d. ſewed.
12. MOORE's DRAMATIC WORKS, with his LIFE, and Four Copper-plates, in 1 vol. 12mo. Price 3s.
13. MOUNT HENNETH, a Novel, in 2 vol. 12mo. Price 7s.
14. MULLIGAN's POEMS on Slavery and Oppreſſion, with Notes and Illuſtrations, in 4to. Price 5s. ſewed.
15. PILGRIM, a Comedy, in Five Acts, performed at the Theatre Royal in Drury Lane, in 8vo. Price 1s. ſewed.
16. POCKET PEERAGE of GREAT BRITAIN and IRELAND, to the Year 1788, with near 1000 Arms, beſides engraved Titles and Frontiſpieces, in 2 vols. 12mo. Price 8s.
17. SENTIMENTAL and DESCRIPTIVE TOUR through the United Provinces, Auſtrian Netherlands, and France, in 2 vols. 12mo. Price 5s. ſewed.
18. STOTHARD's Three Frontiſpieces to EMMA and the SYLPH, each 7 Inches and a half by 6, Price 5s. the Set.
19. YOUNG CLERK's ASSISTANT, on 63 Copper-plates, in 1 vol. royal 8vo. Price 4s. ſewed.

CPSIA information can be obtained
at www.ICGtesting.com
Printed in the USA
BVHW040539101118
532319BV00026B/1812/P